Beautiful
+7 Smash Hits

BEAUTIFUL
CHRISTINA AGUILERA 3

ALL THE THINGS SHE SAID
T.A.T.U. 8

BORN TO TRY
DELTA GOODREM 17

CLOCKS
COLDPLAY 22

CRY ME A RIVER
JUSTIN TIMBERLAKE 28

IF YOU'RE NOT THE ONE
DANIEL BEDINGFIELD 34

SPIRIT IN THE SKY
GARETH GATES 40
(FEATURING THE KUMARS)

TONIGHT
WESTLIFE 44

This publication is not authorised for sale in the
United States of America and / or Canada

Wise Publications
part of The Music Sales Group

London / New York / Paris / Sydney / Copenhagen / Berlin / Madrid / Tokyo

Published by
Wise Publications

Exclusive Distributors:
Music Sales Limited
Distribution Centre, Newmarket Road,
Bury St. Edmunds, Suffolk IP33 3YB, England.
Music Sales Pty Limited
120 Rothschild Avenue, Rosebery, NSW 2018, Australia.

Order No. AM977460
ISBN 1-84449-075-0
This book © Copyright 2003 by Wise Publications.

Unauthorised reproduction of any part of this publication by
any means including photocopying is an infringement of copyright.

Music arranged by Derek Jones.
Music processed by Paul Ewers Music Design.
Cover photographs courtesy of London Features International.
Printed in the United Kingdom by
Printwise (Haverhill) Limited, Haverhill, Suffolk.

Your Guarantee of Quality
As publishers, we strive to produce every book to the highest commercial standards.
The music has been freshly engraved and the book has been carefully designed to minimise
awkward page turns and to make playing from it a real pleasure.
Throughout, the printing and binding have been planned to ensure a sturdy,
attractive publication which should give years of enjoyment.
If your copy fails to meet our high standards, please
inform us and we will gladly replace it.

www.musicsales.com

Beautiful

Words & Music by Linda Perry

© Copyright 2001 Famous Music Corporation, USA.
All Rights Reserved. International Copyright Secured.

All The Things She Said

Words & Music by Sergei Galoyan, Trevor Horn, Martin Kierszenbaum, Elena Kiper & Valerij Polienko

© Copyright 2002 Appleby Music/BMG Music Publishing Limited (25%)/Unforgettable Songs Limited (25%)/
Universal Music Publishing Limited (8.34%)/Copyright Control (41.66%)
All Rights Reserved. International Copyright Secured.

Born To Try

Words & Music by Delta Goodrem & Audius Mtawarira

© Copyright 2003 Sony Music Publishing Australia PTY.
Sony/ATV Music Publishing (UK) Limited.
All Rights Reserved. International Copyright Secured.

Clocks

Words & Music by Guy Berryman, Jon Buckland, Will Champion & Chris Martin

© Copyright 2002 BMG Music Publishing Limited.
Used by permission. All Rights Reserved. International Copyright Secured.

Verse 2:
Confusion that never stops
The closing walls and the ticking clocks
Gonna come back and take you home
I could not stop that you now know, singing…
Come out upon my seas
Cursed missed opportunities
Am I a part of the cure?
Or I am a part of the disease, singing…

You are *etc.*

Cry Me A River

Words & Music by Justin Timberlake, Scott Storch & Tim Mosley

© Copyright 2002 Tennman Tunes/TVT Music Incorporated/Virginia Beach Music.
EMI Music Publishing Limited (25%)/Warner/Chappell Music Limited (25%)/Zomba Music Publishers Limited (50%).
All Rights Reserved. International Copyright Secured.

If You're Not The One

Words & Music by Daniel Bedingfield

[B♭add9] And I'm pray-ing you're the one I build my home with. [E♭9]

[Fsus4] I hope I love you all my life. [E♭sus2] [B♭add9] I don't wan-na run a-way but I

[Cm7add11] can't take it, I don't un-der-stand. [E♭sus2] [B♭add9] If I'm not made for you then why [Cm7add11]

[E♭sus2] does my heart tell me that I am? [Gm7] Is there a-ny way that I can stay [F]

37

in your arms? 'Cause I miss you, body and soul so strong that it takes my breath away. And I breathe you into my heart and pray for the strength to stand today. 'Cause I love you, whether it's wrong or right and though I can't be with you tonight you know my heart is by your side. I don't wan-na run a-way but I can't take it, I don't un-der-stand.

If I'm not made for you then why does my heart tell me that I am?

Is there a-ny way that I can stay in your arms?

Repeat to fade

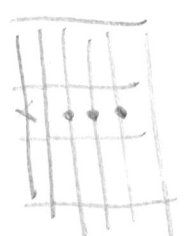

Spirit In The Sky

Words & Music by Norman Greenbaum

♩ = 128

1. When I die and they lay me to rest___ gonna go___ to the place
2. Prepare yourself, you know it's a must, gotta have a friend in Je-
3. Never been a sinner, never sinned. I got a friend in Je-

© Copyright 1969 & 1970 Great Honesty Music Incorporated, USA.
Westminster Music Limited.
All Rights Reserved. International Copyright Secured.

D5
5fr
A5
__ that's the best.__ When I lay me down__ to die, go - ing up__
- sus. So you know that when you die he's
- sus. So you know that when I die he's
2 & 3 time: E5 A5
E5
A5
A5
__ to the spi - rit in the sky. 1,2. Go - ing up__ to the spi -
gon - na re - com - mend you to the spi - rit in the sky. 3. Oh, set me up with the spi -
gon - na set me up with the spi - rit in the sky.
D5
5fr
-rit in the sky.__ That's where I'm gon - na go when I die.__
-rit in the sky.__
A5
E5
To Coda
When I die and they lay me to rest I'm gon - na go to the place__ that's the

best.

Oh,_____ set me up with the spi-rit in the sky.___
-ing on up___ to the spi-rit in the sky.___

E5
That's where I'm gon - na go when I die.
When I die and they
B5
F♯5
1.
lay me to rest I'm gon - na go to the place that's the best.
Go -
2.
best.
Go to the place that's the best.
Go to the place that's the
rit.
B
best.
Go to the place that's the best.
8vb
Drum

Tonight

Words & Music by Steve Mac, Wayne Hector & Jörgen Elofsson

1. Lady I'm so tired, if I took it all out on you. I never meant to. If I left you outside,
2. I don't wanna act like I know that you'll be mine forever though I won't wait forever. Don't want you to feel like

© Copyright 2002 Rokstone Music (33.34%)/Universal Music Publishing Limited (33.33%)/BMG Music Publishing Limited (33.33%).
All Rights Reserved. International Copyright Secured.

if you ev-er felt I ig-nored you. No, my life is all you. So put your
I take you for grant-ed, when-ev-er we are to-geth-er. So put your

best dress on, wrap your-self in the arms of some-one
best dress on, and wrap your-self in the arms of some-one

who wants to give you all the love you want.
who wants to give you all the love you want.

To-night, gon-na make it up to you; to-night.

Gon-na make love to you, to-night, you're gon-na know how much I missed you, ba-by. To-night, I'll de-di-cate my heart to you, to-night, I'm gon-na be a part of you, to-night, you're gon-na know how much I

1. miss you, I miss you so.

2. miss you and I miss you

so.

So put your best dress on, wrap your-self in my arms my love. To-night, gon-na make it up to you; to-night gon-na make love to you to-night, you're gon-na know how much I miss you, ba - by. To-

- night, I'll de-di-cate my heart to you,_ to - night,_ I'm gon-na be a part_ of you,_ to - night,_

you're gon-na know how much I miss_ you ba - by. To-

miss_ you, and I miss you_ so._